Prayers for Children Who Are Starting School
Children's Christian Prayer Books

BABY PROFESSOR
EDUCATION KIDS

Reciting a prayer before studying is a delightful act that will make children feel the importance of attending school.

It is like
introducing
them to the
great wisdom
of God.

Children, these
prayers will give
you strength
and wisdom
to be good in
school and to
become great
children of God.

A Prayer for School

Dear Lord, Almighty Father
Give me protection as I
begin to gain wisdom
And knowledge, I offer you my days
Guide all the children like me
Guide all the teachers
That they will treat as their own
And to love us unconditionally
And to accept our imperfections
Like the way You do. Amen.

A Prayer for School

Dear Lord, Almighty Father
Give me protection as I
begin to gain wisdom
And knowledge, I offer you my days
Guide all the children like me
Guide all the teachers
That they will treat as their own
And to love us unconditionally
And to accept our imperfections
Like the way You do. Amen.

Prayer to Jesus

Jesus, we praise you
for this lovely day
As we set our feet towards school
Make this day the beginning
of a great journey
With You Jesus, being the
great teacher of all
We know that learning in school
Will be a great experience
To make us unique children of God
Worthy of Your love
and mercy. Amen.

Prayer to Jesus

Jesus, we praise you for this lovely day
As we set our feet towards school
Make this day the beginning
of a great journey
With You Jesus, being the
great teacher of all
We know that learning in school
Will be a great experience
To make us unique children of God
Worthy of Your love and mercy. Amen.

Jesus as my Classmate
As I set my way to school
I know I will be in a perfect place
Of great love, creativity, and wisdom
It will be a great place
Where I know Jesus more
For He will always be
My seatmate and my classmate
Who will encourage me when
lessons are difficult,
Who will teach me the value
of respect and love,
Who will guide me towards
the path of excellence.

Jesus as my Classmate
As I set my way to school
I know I will be in a perfect place
Of great love, creativity, and wisdom
It will be a great place
Where I know Jesus more
For He will always be
My seatmate and my classmate
Who will encourage me when
lessons are difficult,
Who will teach me the value
of respect and love,
Who will guide me towards
the path of excellence.

Prayer Before Class

Dear Heavenly Father,
Thank you for sending me to school,
Fulfil my day with Your truth and love
Give me courage when things get hard
Be my strength when I'm about to give up,
Your peace and greatness
Inspire me to strive hard
and to be good
Inspire my teachers and make them as
Meaningful instruments to spread
Great wisdom and love. Amen.

Prayer Before Class

Dear Heavenly Father,

Thank you for sending me to school,

Fulfil my day with Your truth and love

Give me courage when things get hard

Be my strength when I'm

about to give up,

Your peace and greatness

Inspire me to strive hard and to be good

Inspire my teachers and make them as

Meaningful instruments to spread

Great wisdom and love. Amen.

REWRITE THE SENTENCES.

Prayer for Guidance

Dear Lord Jesus, I pray
that may study hard
Inspire me more when
things are hard for me
Be my guide in quest for
knowledge and wisdom
Organize my thoughts
and enrich my skills
Make each day a meaningful
learning opportunity
Let me focus on my studies
as I should be.

REWRITE THE SENTENCES.

Prayer for Guidance

Dear Lord Jesus, I pray

that may study hard

Inspire me more when

things are hard for me

Be my guide in quest for

knowledge and wisdom

Organize my thoughts and enrich my skills

Make each day a meaningful

learning opportunity

Let me focus on my studies

as I should be.

REWRITE THE SENTENCES.

Prayer for School

Dear Lord Jesus,
Be my special friend
I pray that You will be with
me towards the end,
Be my guiding light
As I study through the night,
You are my source of
love and inspiration
Make me a worthy fellow as
part of Your creation.
Amen.

Prayer for School

Dear Lord Jesus,
Be my special friend
I pray that You will be with
me towards the end,
Be my guiding light
As I study through the night,
You are my source of love and inspiration
Make me a worthy fellow as
part of Your creation.
Amen.

REWRITE THE SENTENCES.

A Thanksgiving Prayer

Lord Jesus thank you for
sending me here
Make it a day of great
fun and friendship
Thank you for the opportunity
To learn new things and
to explore each day
Make us love one another,
Thank you for each time
of learning together,
Amen.

REWRITE THE SENTENCES.

A Thanksgiving Prayer

Lord Jesus thank you for
sending me here
Make it a day of great fun and friendship
Thank you for the opportunity
To learn new things and
to explore each day
Make us love one another,
Thank you for each time
of learning together.
Amen.

REWRITE THE SENTENCES.

Prayer for Study Time

Heavenly Father, fill each
new learning day
With great love, fun,
friendship, and opportunity
To be with other children and
to be with my teachers,
As we study together our lessons,
make each one the bearers,
Of Your love, truth and wisdom
To make our learning environment
just like your kingdom.
Amen.

REWRITE THE SENTENCES.

Prayer for Study Time

Heavenly Father, fill each

new learning day

With great love, fun, friendship,

and opportunity

To be with other children and

to be with my teachers,

As we study together our lessons,

make each one the bearers,

Of Your love, truth and wisdom

To make our learning environment

just like your kingdom.

Amen.

Visit
BABY PROFESSOR
EDUCATION KIDS
www.BabyProfessorBooks.com
to download Free Baby Professor eBooks
and view our catalog of new and exciting
Children's Books